# Xtreme Sports

# Motocross

Aaron Carr

AV2

www.av2books.com

## Step 1
Go to **www.av2books.com**

## Step 2
Enter this unique code

**OVDWJ4FZQ**

## Step 3
Explore your interactive eBook!

Xtreme Sports

**Motocross**

**Start!**

**AV2 is optimized for use on any device**

# Your interactive eBook comes with...

**Read**

**Audio**
Listen to the entire
book read aloud

**Videos**
Watch informative
video clips

**Weblinks**
Gain additional
information for research

**Try This!**
Complete activities and
hands-on experiments

**Key Words**
Study vocabulary, and
complete a matching
word activity

**Quizzes**
Test your knowledge

**Slideshows**
View images and captions

**View new titles and product videos at
www.av2books.com**

# Motocross

## Contents

Motocross is a sport. People ride motorbikes over jumps and along a track.

5

**Motocross bikes are small and light. They are made for going over jumps and racing on dirt tracks.**

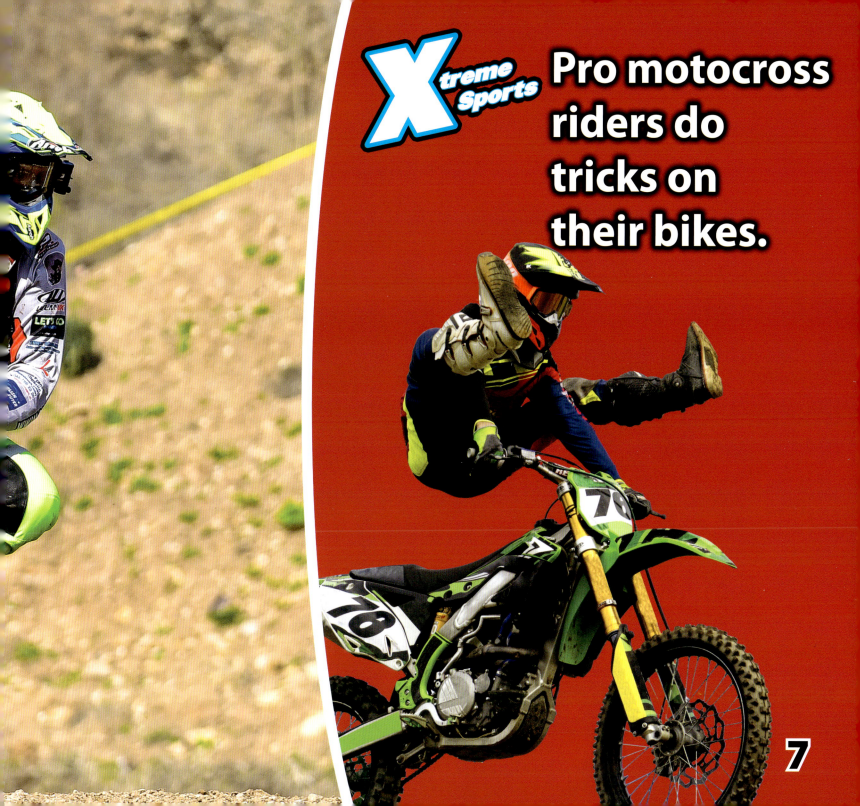

**Pro motocross riders do tricks on their bikes.**

Motocross riders should always wear a helmet. Helmets keep riders safe when they fall.

8

Pro motocross riders wear motocross suits to keep them safe.

People ride motocross bikes on dirt tracks. These tracks can be in the woods or in a place made for motocross.

Pro motocross riders drive on tracks with big ramps.

**Practice is very important. Riders must practice often to become good at motocross.**

**Pro motocross riders practice for many hours each day.**

**Motocross riders jump off a ramp and do a trick. This is called Best Trick.**

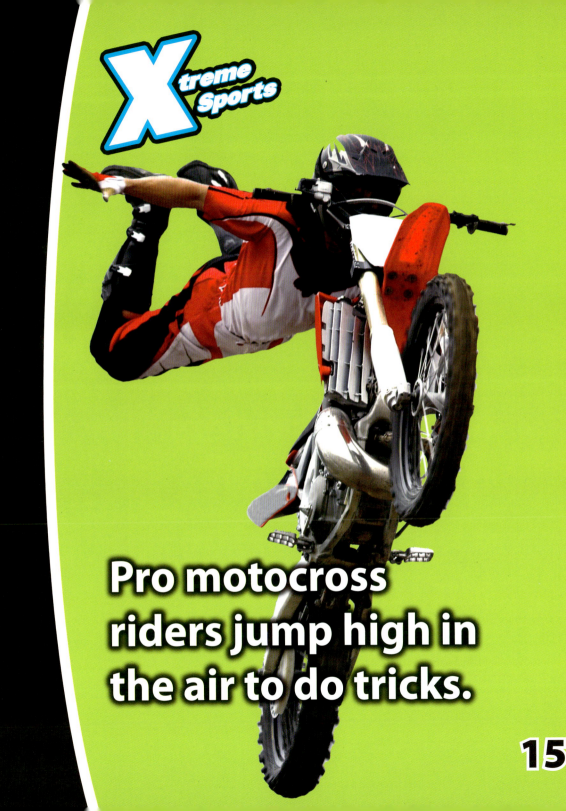

**Pro motocross riders jump high in the air to do tricks.**

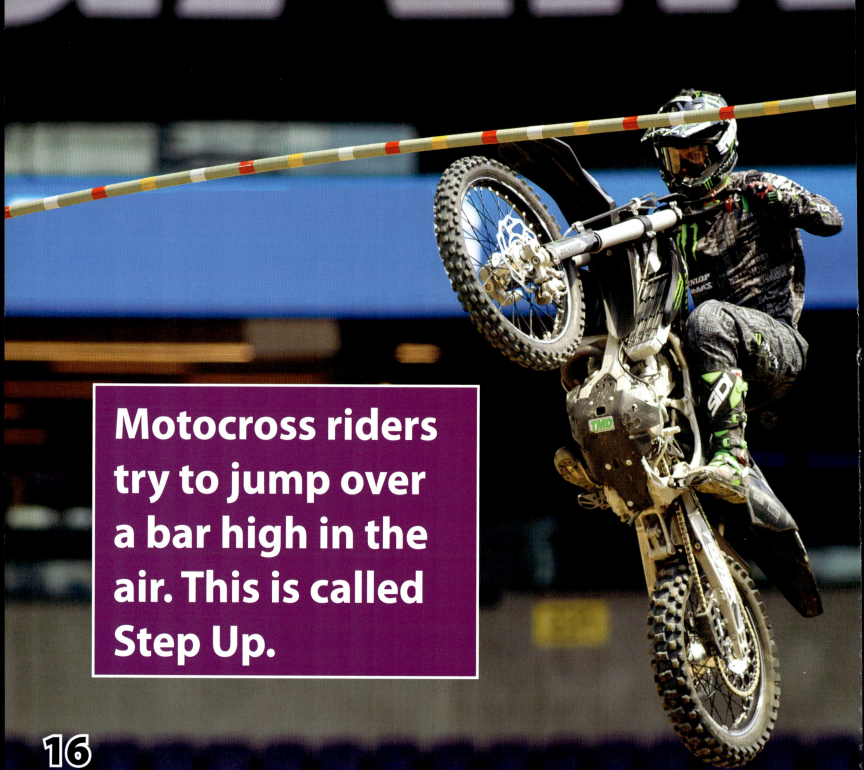

**Motocross riders try to jump over a bar high in the air. This is called Step Up.**

**Pro motocross riders try to jump as high as they can.**

**Motocross riders race around a course with three kinds of track. This is called Supermoto.**

18

**Motocross riders drive fast to finish the race first.**

Great motocross riders from around the world come to the X Games each year.

They do big jumps and tricks in front of large crowds.

# MOTOCROSS FACTS

These pages provide detailed information that expands on the interesting facts found in this book. These pages are intended to be used by adults as a learning support to help young readers round out their knowledge of each sport in the *Extreme Sports* series.

**Pages 4–5**

**Motocross is a sport that requires skill, determination, and balance.** Riders use specially designed motorcycles to race around dirt tracks and over obstacles. Sometimes, riders perform tricks such as flips and jumps. Motocross is based on a British off-road sport called scrambles, which began in 1924.

**Pages 6–7**

**Motocross bikes are designed to be lightweight and very durable.** They must be able to withstand the extreme forces caused by landing high jumps. These bikes are smaller than normal motorcycles and have smaller, louder engines. In order to keep their weight down, motocross bikes do not have speedometers, lights, or even kickstands. The seat is long and flat to allow riders to change position during tricks.

**Pages 8–9**

**The helmet is the most important piece of safety equipment.** When falling off a motorcycle, the rider's head may hit the ground. Helmets have saved many riders from serious head injuries. Motocross riders also wear motocross suits, padded gloves and boots, and chest protectors to keep them safe. Their helmets feature a full face shield and goggles to protect the face and eyes.

**Pages 10–11**

**Freestyle motocross can be done anywhere there is plenty of open space and dirt.** Natural tracks can be found on public land and may have dirt and rock ramps, hills, and jumps. Some riders build their own tracks. Pro motocross tracks are built for safety and to allow riders to reach great heights for tricks. The tracks include ramps with landing areas, dirt piled into hills and bumps, and padded bumpers for safety.

**Practice is the most important part of becoming good at any sport.** Most professional motocross riders practice for many hours every day. They push themselves to improve their skills by trying new tricks and riding styles. Some motocross riders try to invent new tricks. They must practice these tricks many times to ensure they can repeat the moves properly in competitions.

**Best Trick is one of the most extreme motocross competitions.** Ten riders each take two jumps off a dirt-covered ramp. After launching off the ramp, riders perform tricks in the air and land on another dirt ramp that helps them slow down. Tricks include backflips, front flips, and corkscrews. Riders are judged on style and the difficulty of the trick.

**The Step Up competition is a high jump event for motocross riders.** Two vertical bars are set on top of a wall of dirt. A horizontal bar is then laid between the two bars at a height of 26 to 29 feet (8 to 9 meters). Riders take turns riding off a ramp to jump over the bar. If they cannot clear the bar, they are eliminated. The bar is raised 6 inches (15 centimeters) each round. The event continues until only one rider is left.

**Supermoto is a combination of motocross and road racing.** Supermoto courses feature three types of track—flat dirt track, motocross style dirt track with jumps and bumps, and smooth pavement. The layout of the track changes often, and it is filled with obstacles throughout. Riders must navigate dirt and steel jumps, high-speed straightaways, and twisting corners on their way to the finish line.

**The Summer X Games is an annual sports tournament that showcases the best athletes in the extreme sports world.** The X Games started in 1995. The competition includes events for BMX, skateboarding, and motocross. These games attract the best extreme athletes from around the world each year. Some events feature athletes flying 40 feet (12 m) above the ground.

# KEY WORDS

Research has shown that as much as 65 percent of all written material published in English is made up of 300 words. These 300 words cannot be taught using pictures or learned by sounding them out. They must be recognized by sight. This book contains 57 common sight words to help young readers improve their reading fluency and comprehension. This book also teaches young readers several important content words, such as proper nouns. These words are paired with pictures to aid in learning and improve understanding.

| Page | Sight Words First Appearance |
|------|------------------------------|
| 5 | a, along, and, is, over, people |
| 6 | are, for, light, made, on, small, they |
| 7 | do, their |
| 8 | always, keep, should, when |
| 9 | them, to |
| 10 | be, can, in, or, place, the, these |
| 11 | big, with |
| 12 | at, good, important, must, often, very |
| 13 | day, each, many |
| 14 | off, this |
| 15 | air, high |
| 16 | try, up |
| 17 | as |
| 18 | around, kinds, of, three |
| 19 | first |
| 21 | come, from, great, large, world, year |

| Page | Content Words First Appearance |
|------|--------------------------------|
| 5 | jumps, motocross, motorbikes, sport, track |
| 6 | bikes |
| 7 | riders, tricks |
| 8 | helmet |
| 9 | suits |
| 10 | woods |
| 11 | ramps |
| 12 | practice |
| 13 | hours |
| 14 | Best Trick |
| 16 | bar, Step Up |
| 18 | course, Supermoto |
| 19 | race |
| 21 | crowds, X Games |

Published by AV2
14 Penn Plaza, 9th Floor  New York, NY 10122
Website: www.av2books.com

Library of Congress Control Number: 2020935081

ISBN 978-1-7911-2684-1 (hardcover)
ISBN 978-1-7911-2685-8 (softcover)
ISBN 978-1-7911-2686-5 (multi-user eBook)
ISBN 978-1-7911-2687-2 (single-user eBook)

Printed in Guangzhou, China
1 2 3 4 5 6 7 8 9 0  24 23 22 21 20

052020
100919

Art Director: Terry Paulhus  Project Coordinator: Ryan Smith

Every reasonable effort has been made to trace ownership and to obtain permission to reprint copyright material. The publisher would be pleased to have any errors or omissions brought to its attention so that they may be corrected in subsequent printings.

The publisher acknowledges Getty Images, iStock, and Shutterstock as the primary image suppliers for this title.